j811   c.1
R25m
Reece, Colleen L.
My first Christmas book.

Holiday Shelf

E.R

MY FIRST CHRISTMAS BOOK

by Colleen L. Reece
illustrated by Linda Hohag

created by The Child's World

 CHILDRENS PRESS ™

CHICAGO

Library of Congress Cataloging in Publication Data

Reece, Colleen L.
  My first Christmas book.

  Summary: Focuses on themes associated
with Christmas, including decorations, presents, cookies,
and Santa Claus.
  1. Christmas—Juvenile poetry.   2. Children's
poetry, American.   [1. Christmas—Poetry.   2. American
poetry] I. Hohag, Linda, ill.   II. Child's World (Firm)
III. Title.
PS3568.E3646M9   1984   811'.54   84-7816
ISBN 0-516-02901-0

MY FIRST

CHRISTMAS
BOOK

A Christmas Tree

I helped Dad pick out our Christmas tree.
"Here's one," I said. "It's beautiful!"
"Yes," said Dad. "But it's too tall."

"Look, Dad. This one isn't tall."
"No," he said, "But it's too fat."

"This one isn't fat."

"But it's too small."

I looked and looked.
Then I saw a tree that
   wasn't too tall,
   wasn't too fat, and
   wasn't too small.
"Dad! Dad! I found it!"
"Yes," he said. "That one's
   just right."

— *Marie Frost*

Tree Trimming

Monday we popped popcorn.
Tuesday we made strings.
Wednesday we bought shiny balls
   and pretty Christmas things.
Thursday we got out the star. . .
   and Dad put up the tree!
Tonight we're decorating it,
   Jeremiah
     and
       me.

Decorations

Candles in windows
  that shine on the snow,
Wreaths of green branches
  and red satin bows,
Tinsel and holly
  that glisten and glow—
    Christmas is coming.
    My eyes tell me so!

A Snowman

Dancing white snowflakes
play tag
       c
        o
         m
        i   d
        n   o
        g   w
              n,

chasing each other
from sky to the ground—
spreading a blanket
all over my town.

I roll giant snowballs
until they are hard,
and make a big Santa
to stand in my yard.

A Christmas Play

Guess what!
I'm the Christmas angel
   in our play.
Last year I was the "a"
   in Merry Christmas.
This year is lots better.
I wear a sparkly white dress,
   and silver wings
      and tinsel in my hair.
I'd rather be an angel
      than an " a."

Cookies

Trees and stars,
Santas and elves,
Angels and snowmen,
Bows and bells.
Mom and I make them
    from cookie dough—
put them in the oven
    and watch them
    G R O W!

16

One Peek

Packages lumpy,
    and bumpy,
       and wide—
I find I'm wondering what's
      hiding
        inside.
Tricycles, bicycles, drums
      that make noise?
Huggable pandas for
    girls and
      for boys?
I'm waiting for Christmas—
    but it's still a *whole week*!
Would anyone mind if I took
    just
      one peek?

—*Marie Frost*

Candy Canes

Candy canes
   are like peppermint sticks.
The more I lick them
   the smaller they get!

When I'm done
   and get ready for bed,
I stick out my tongue
   and it's candy cane red!

Sleigh Bells

Reindeer prancing through the snow.
Sleigh bells jingling as they go.
Now I know that Santa's near.
This is what I hear:
   Tap, tap, tap!
   Thump, thump, thump!
   Then,
   down the chimney
   with a bump!
I will not move.
I will not peep!
For Santa thinks
I'm fast asleep!

—Jane Belk Moncure

Stockings

When Santa stuffs our stockings
   all hanging in a row—
one little elf climbs down inside
   to stuff each stocking toe.
Then Santa fills them to the top
   before he says "Heigh-ho".
One Christmas Eve I saw it—
   that is how I know!

—Jane Belk Moncure

A Special Tree

Outside, the birds had a
   Christmas tree,
but its branches were cold
   and bare—
not a colored light,
not a paper chain,
not a present anywhere.

So we made the birds
   a Christmas tree
with gifts of food to share.
For Christmas is a giving time,
   a time to say, "We care."

—Jane Belk Moncure

A Caring Time

Caring for others is what
   Christmas is about.
When Baby's sleeping—trying
   not to shout.
Finding my shoes
   so Mom won't have to look.
Setting the table, helping Mom cook.
Rocking the baby when I'd rather play,
   realizing Mother has had a bad day.
Mother says I have done all
   that I could
   to make Christmas special,
   because I've been good.

—*Marie Frost*

A Christmas Story

Christmas stories are fun.
  My favorite is
    about the baby Jesus.
He lay
  on the hay.
    Cows and sheep
      watched him sleep.
A little donkey stood nearby.
A special star was in the sky.

Caroling

It's Christmas time!
  It's Christmas time!
We sing the songs of Christmas time.
Jingle bells jingle
  and candles glow
as we go caroling in the snow.
"We wish you a Merry Christmas
  and a Happy New Year!"